W9-BSK-458

To

From

Date

WHY AM I HERE, ANYWAY?

ANTHONY DeSTEFANO

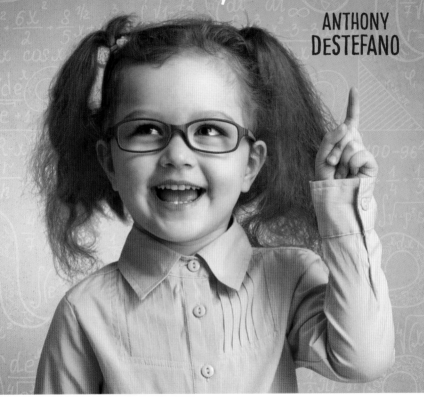

HARVEST HOUSE PUBLISHERS

EUGENE, OREGON

WHY AM I HERE, ANYWAY?

Published by Harvest House Publishers
Eugene, Oregon 97402
www.harvesthousepublishers.com

978-0-7369-6469-2 (hardcover)
978-0-7369-6470-8 (ebook)

Design and production by Left Coast Design
Cover photo © Clint Scholz /iStockphoto
All other photos © AdobeStock

Digital photo editing by Schmalen Design, Inc.

Scripture quotations are taken from...

the New American Standard Bible®, © 1960, 1962, 1963, 1968, 1971, 1972, 1973, 1975, 1977, 1995 by The Lockman Foundation. Used by permission. (www.Lockman.org)

the Holy Bible, New International Version®, NIV®. Copyright © 1973, 1978, 1984, 2011 by Biblica, Inc.® Used by permission. All rights reserved worldwide.

Printed in China
16 17 18 19 20 21 22 23 24 25 / LP / 10 9 8 7 6 5 4 3 2 1

This book is dedicated to

Laura and Curt Ciumei

Do you sometimes feel that you've lost your way?
That you're alone in a dark forest—unsure of how
to find your way out, or what life is about?

Do you ever just wonder,
Why am I here, anyway?

Can it be that this is really all there is to life?
Paying bills, dealing with problems,
struggling to get by?

We hear people say all the time that everyone is "special." But is that really true? Sure, there are certain individuals who seem special—geniuses, heroes,

celebrities, and saints—all the people who have
somehow managed to stand out from the crowd.

But what about the rest of humanity—
all those nameless individuals who are completely
unknown, unappreciated, unsuccessful, and unhappy?
Are they special too?

And what about us? I don't know about you,
but I don't look special. I don't feel special.
I'm just, well...average.

And yet, according to science,
you and I are *very* special.

Not only do we have our own
unique fingerprints and genetic code...

but just think of all the possible combinations
of DNA that could have resulted when our parents
first conceived us—think of the incalculable odds we had
to overcome just to be born. Over *half a billion* potential
human beings—each one completely different from
us—could have been born in our place.

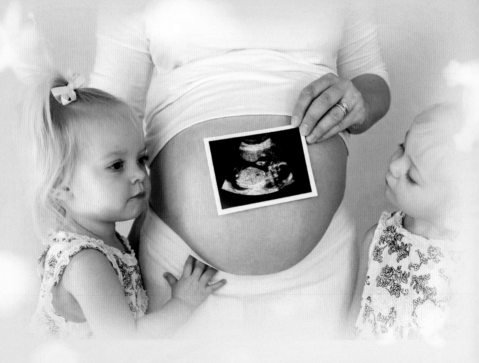

No matter how average you may feel, it's just a scientific
fact that you came into this world a winner.
Victory was your starting point.

And what about the human spirit? Throughout the Bible there are so many references to the fact that God was aware of our existence *before* He created us:

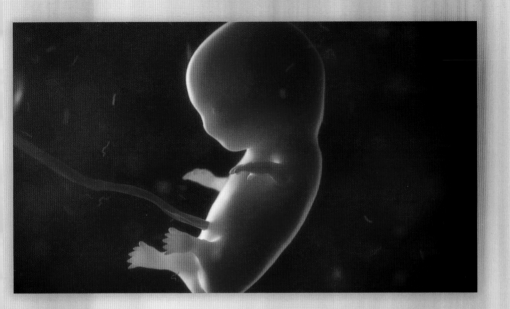

"Before I formed you in the womb I knew you, and before you were born I consecrated you."

JEREMIAH 1:5

"All the days ordained for me were written in your book before one of them came to be."

PSALM 139:16

"He chose us in Him before the foundation of the world."

EPHESIANS 1:4

All of this points to one
inescapable conclusion:
God had us in mind even before we existed
and even before the earth was created. Therefore
He *must* have something special planned for us.

And that's where the solution to the mystery lies. We live in such a broken, fallen world— a world badly in need of fixing.

Our God is a master craftsman. In fact, He was
a carpenter once. He knows all about the problems we
face. And He chose us to be His special instruments
to fix some part of this crazy, broken world.

Each of us is special because there is a special
mission for each of us to accomplish. There is some
unique problem in the universe that *only we* can solve.

In the end, we're not just human beings, but *keys*—
keys that God has individually crafted to fit certain locks.
In all the world and in all of time itself, there has only been
one key that has the ability to open one particular lock—
one key to solve one particular problem.

And YOU
are it!

When you find the lock,
you find your mission.

When you turn the key,
you unlock your destiny.

And the amazing thing is,
it could be anything—

something big...

or something small...

something that makes you famous overnight...

or something that keeps you hidden.

You might be destined to *save*
someone's life by being heroic...

or *change* someone's life
with a simple conversation.

You might invent
something that
transforms the world...

or maybe have a son or daughter who will.

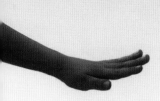

Whatever it turns out to be, one thing is certain: In the eyes of God, it will be something great. And to you—personally—it will be something deeply fulfilling.

So how do you find this key to the
meaning and purpose of your life?

According to the Bible,
there's only one way.

ONE WAY

By asking God!
Does that sound too simple?
It's not!

"Ask and it will be given to you;
seek and you will find;
knock and the door will
be opened to you."

Matthew 7:7

If you ask God every day, He will point you
in the right direction. He will guide you step-
by-step. He will *lead you* to your destiny.

But you have to sit still and listen!

Don't worry about all the obstacles you need to overcome—just concentrate on being *led by God.*

Be clay in His hands—not marble.

Marble is hard, resistant to change, unmovable.
In order for God to sculpt anything wonderful
with marble, He has to chop pieces off with a
hammer and chisel—and that can be painful!

But if you're clay, He can be gentle.
He can mold you softly—and quickly.

So be open to anything God wants.
Be clay. Every morning when you wake up,
humbly ask God, *Please lead me to my destiny.*

Do that every single day—and then just *trust* Him.

Be sorry when you fall.

Be thankful instead
of spoiled.

Prayerful instead of prideful.

Devote your
life to serving
others and not
yourself.

Worship God and not yourself.

In short, be *in union* with God.

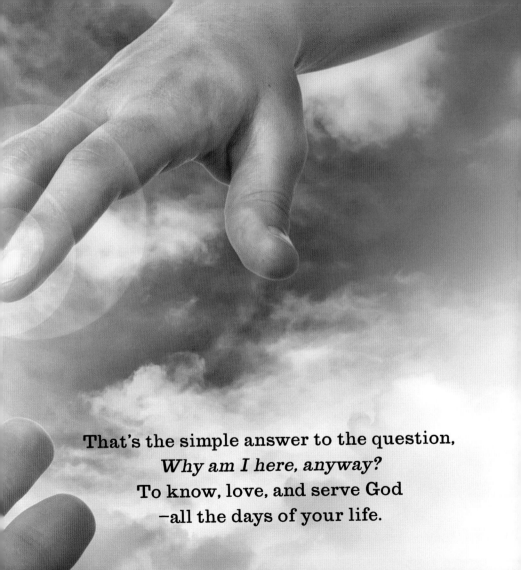

That's the simple answer to the question,
Why am I here, anyway?
To know, love, and serve God
—all the days of your life.

When you're in union with God,
you're on the fast track to achieving
your purpose in life—to unlocking the key
to the problem in the universe that
you alone are destined to solve.

It doesn't matter if you're young or old,

rich or poor,

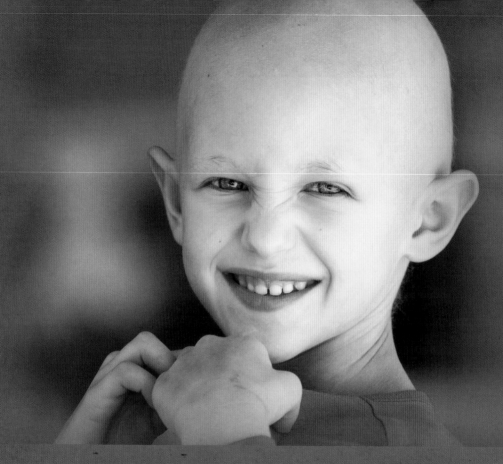

healthy or sick.

All you have to do is ask God,
and He will lead you.

And do you know what else He will do?
Not only will He reveal to you your true purpose,
but little by little, He will transform your whole
life into a spectacular adventure.

And even after your life is complete, even after you've taken your last breath and your heart has stopped beating—even then the great adventure will not be over. Because when you open your eyes again in the world to come, the One who gave you life will look at you and say,

"*Well done, good and faithful servant... enter into the joy of your master.*"

MATTHEW 25:21